The Sioux

ANNA KOOPMANS

PRINCIPAL PHOTOGRAPHY BY MARILYN "ANGEL" WYNN

CHELSEA CLUBHOUSE

An Imprint of Chelsea House Publishers

A Haights Cross Communications Company

Philadelphia

This edition first published in 2004 in the United States of America by Chelsea Clubhouse, a division of Chelsea House Publishers and a subsidiary of Haights Cross Communications.

Chelsea Clubhouse
1974 Sproul Road, Suite 400
Broomall, PA 19008-0914

The Chelsea House world wide web address is www.chelseahouse.com

Library of Congress Cataloging-in-Publication Data

Koopmans, Anna.
  The Sioux / Anna Koopmans.
     v. cm. -- (American Indian art and culture)
Includes bibliographical references and index.
Contents: The people -- Sioux homes -- Sioux communities -- Sioux clothing -- Sioux food -- Tools and technology -- Sioux religion -- Ceremonies and celebrations -- Music and dance -- Language and storytelling -- Sioux art -- Special feature -- Studying the Sioux's past.
  ISBN 0-7910-7963-5 (Chelsea House) (lib. bdg. : alk. paper)
 1. Dakota Indians--History--Juvenile literature. 2. Dakota Indians--Social life and customs--Juvenile literature. [1. Dakota Indians.] I. Title. II. Series.
  E99.D1K66 2004
  978.004'7524--dc22
                                    2003017531
                        Printed in the United States of America
                        1 2 3 4 5 6 7 8 9 0 07 06 05 04 03

Project Coordinator Heather C. Hudak **Substantive Editor** Donald Wells **Design** Janine Vangool **Layout** Terry Paulhus **Photo Researcher** Wendy Cosh **Chelsea Clubhouse Editors** Sally Cheney and Margaret Brierton **Validator** Susana D. Geliga

Cover: Sioux Pine Ridge (Marilyn "Angel" Wynn), Greg Red Elk (Marilyn "Angel" Wynn), Fancy Shawl Dancer (Kit Breen), Sioux Beadwork (Marilyn "Angel" Wynn); Kit Breen: page 21R; Courtesy of Donald F. Montileaux: page 27; Cheryl Richter: pages 3, 17, 19, 29; Marilyn "Angel" Wynn: pages 1, 4, 5, 6, 7, 8, 9, 10, 11T, 11B, 12, 13, 14T, 14B, 15, 16, 18, 20, 21L, 22, 23, 24T, 24B, 25, 26, 28T, 28B, 30, 31.

Please note
At the time of printing, the Internet addresses appearing in this book were correct. Owing to the dynamic nature of the Internet, however, we cannot guarantee that all these addresses will remain correct.

CONTENTS

The People

The Sioux are one of many American Indian nations who lived in the midwest region of North America. The Sioux did not always live on the Great Plains. Early European explorers first met the Sioux in northwest Wisconsin and central Minnesota. This area has many lakes and forests. Here, the Sioux grew crops, such as corn and squash, and gathered the wild rice that grew in the wetlands. They also hunted woodland animals such as deer and elk. They made clay pottery containers and lived in lodges made of tree poles, bark, and dirt. In the mid-1600s, the Sioux began moving south and west toward the Great Plains. The Sioux moved for many reasons. In the Northwest, the Sioux faced conflicts with the Ojibwa. They were also crowded by the arrival of the European settlers. However, they could look forward to finding a large amount of wildlife on the Great Plains. This wildlife could be used for food and clothing.

As the Sioux moved west to the Great Plains, they settled in different regions along the Minnesota River in present-day Wyoming, Montana, and North and South Dakota.

The tipi was the most common type of Sioux dwelling. The tipi was made from poles and buffalo hides.

Over time, three different language **dialects** emerged among the Sioux: the Dakota, Lakota, and Nakota, all of which mean "allies," or "friends." Together, the Dakota, Lakota, and Nakota groups are known as the Great Sioux Nation.

In the past, the Sioux were **nomadic**, following **bison** herds over the Great Plains. Today, many Sioux live in towns and cities. Others still live on **reservations** in South Dakota, North Dakota, Minnesota, Montana, and Nebraska.

The Sioux have not forgotten their traditional way of life. Many work hard to pass on stories, dances, crafts, and customs to their children.

The Europeans introduced horses to the Sioux in the 1700s. Horses enabled the Sioux to travel long distances faster than they could on foot. European settlers also brought new diseases that made some of the Sioux very sick, and many of them died. Europeans began settling the land by building forts and railways. Conflicts between the Sioux and the Europeans developed. The Sioux fought to protect their rights and their land. In the end, the European settlers could not be stopped. The Sioux were forced onto reservations.

Sioux Map

Location of Sioux reservations in South Dakota

Standing Rock
Grande River
Lake Traverse
Moreau River
Cheyenne River
L. Oahe
South Dakota
Belle Fourche R.
Cheyenne River
Pierre
L. Sharpe
Crow Creek
Flandreau
Mount Rushmore N MEM
Badlands NP
White River
Jewel Cave NM
Wind Cave NP
White River
Pine Ridge River
Rosebud
Yankton

N

Sioux Homes

Traditionally, the Great Plains Sioux lived in **tipis**. The tipi was shaped like a cone and made with bison hides and long tree poles. The long tree poles were leaned against each other and tied at the top. Bison hides were stretched over the poles. The Sioux needed homes that would suit their way of life. Tipis were easy to build and easy to move.

In the summer months, the tipi hides could be rolled up to allow fresh air inside. All tipis had a small doorway opening that was covered with a bison hide. Wood or bone pins held the doorway in place.

When the Sioux moved their villages, the long poles from the tipi were dragged behind their horses and used to carry belongings. The device made from the poles was called a travois.

DWELLING AND DECORATION

In the center of the tipi, the Sioux built a hearth, or fire pit, for cooking and heating. Two flaps at the top of the tipi opened to release smoke from the hearth. The flaps could also be closed to keep out rain, snow, or wind. Stones and wooden stakes held down the bottom of the tipi.

Sioux women helped make the tipis. They prepared bison hides in a process known as **tanning**. First, the women stretched the hides and scraped them clean using tools made from bones or elk antlers. They soaked the hides in water for several days. Then they rubbed animal fats and animal brains into the hides to make them soft. They washed and softened the hides once more. Finally, the hides were smoked over a low fire to make them waterproof.

Bison hide was staked to the ground to stretch it. Once the hide was stretched and treated, it could be used to cover tipis. It could also be decorated and used for clothing.

Today, the Sioux make their homes in cities, towns, farms, and reservations. Many Sioux return to their reservations for traditional celebrations and ceremonies. Sioux often use tipis for **wacipi** and camping. Tipis are also used at special events such as rodeos.

Sioux Communities

Traditional Sioux communities were built around family members and relatives. Each generation was taught to respect its elders. They were taught to live in harmony with one another and with nature.

The Sioux's survival depended on everyone doing his or her job. Sioux men had many different jobs. Some were hunters. Others were scouts who found bison and other wild animals. These men worked together to find meat and hides. The warriors helped keep the tribe safe. There were also storytellers who reminded the community about their history and religious beliefs.

The traditional Sioux way of life was based on hunting. They lived in tipis that were easy to pack up and move to new hunting locations.

Men performed specific tasks as part of their daily lives. The skills they displayed in these tasks earned them respect among the tribe. They were recognized for their healing powers, hunting skills, courage as warriors, wisdom in settling arguments, or skill in trade with other tribes.

For the most part, all Sioux men were equal. However, each Sioux community had a tribal chief. The tribal chief was a well-respected man who represented the tribe at important events such as war councils, trade meetings, and treaty signings. Men held most of the power in the tribe. They represented their families at all tribal talks. Women did not take part in tribal meetings; however, a man's wife was free to voice her opinion.

Women gathered vegetables and fruits and collected firewood. They also prepared food, made clothing, and built tipis. Women owned the tipis and everything inside them. Women were respected because they were givers of life, they took care of the children, and sometimes they led ceremonies.

Through close relationships in the Sioux community, children were taught to be kind to others.

Sioux children did not attend school. Every day, they learned valuable lessons and skills from family members. Girls learned to tan hides and cook food, while boys learned to hunt using bows and arrows.

Most parents arranged marriages for their children. During the marriage ceremony, the families of the bride and groom exchanged gifts as a sign of friendship and respect.

Sioux Clothing

The Sioux had two types of clothing. They wore one type for daily tasks. They wore the other type for special occasions or ceremonies.

The Sioux made their clothing from tanned deer or elk hides. Women wore knee-length dresses. They also wore leggings that reached to the knee. Men wore sleeveless shirts and breechcloths, which are similar to short pants. In the winter, men wore leggings and bison robes.

For the Fancy Dance, men wear brightly colored feather bustles.

Sioux men and women had many different ways to decorate their clothing. They often wore jewelry, such as colorful bone necklaces and armbands, which were decorated with beads. At five or six years of age, children had their ears pierced. In addition, for special celebrations, successful warriors wore feathers in their headbands. Women used their knowledge of making dyes to paint or tattoo designs on their faces and bodies. Warriors and hunters painted their faces and the halters of their horses with bright colors. The beautiful designs they painted were thought to encourage the support of important spirits.

The Sioux wore animal hide shoes called **moccasins**. Moccasins were often decorated with colorful quillwork or beadwork. Each tribe had its own style of decoration.

Sometimes the Sioux decorated their bodies for religious reasons. Sioux men believed that wearing a single eagle feather gave them the bird's strength and bravery. They also believed the Great Spirit would help and protect them when they wore an eagle feather. The eagle feather could be worn in their hair or as part of a headdress. Headdresses made of many eagle feathers were worn only on special occasions, such as a **Sun Dance** or during treaty meetings. Today, the headdress is still considered special and it is worn at events such as tribal meetings and wacipi.

Sioux Food

At one time, millions of bison roamed the Great Plains. Bison was the Sioux's most important food source. The Sioux boiled bison meat with wild vegetables such as turnips or onions. They added wild berries for extra flavor. They also roasted the meat on a stick over a fire or cut it into strips and placed it on racks to dry. Dried meat would not spoil for a long time. Sioux men also hunted antelope, deer, and elk for food.

It was difficult to find food during the winter. Sioux men hunted in the summer and fall when the bison were fat. Many of the Great Plains Indians, including the Sioux, made pemmican. Pemmican was made of dried meat that was pounded into powder and mixed with melted animal fat and berries. The Sioux ate pemmican during the long winter because it would not spoil.

Horses arrived in the 1700s, making it easier for the Sioux to hunt. Hunters could travel greater distances to find bison. European settlers also brought many food items to the Sioux. The Sioux learned to use these new ingredients, such as flour, sugar, baking soda, seasonings, and coffee, along with their traditional food.

The Sioux dried meat by cutting it into small strips and hanging it on racks or sinew lines to dry.

Indian Fry Bread

Ingredients:

2 cups (574 ml) flour

3 teaspoons (15 ml) baking powder

1 teaspoon (5 ml) salt

1 cup (237 ml) milk

oil for frying

Equipment:

large bowl

wooden spoon

frying pan, deep fryer, or wok

slotted spoon

sifter

Directions

1. Sift flour and baking powder together in a bowl.

2. Slowly stir in milk. Add more flour as necessary to make the dough less sticky.

3. Coat your hands and the tabletop with flour.

4. Knead the dough until it is smooth. The dough should not stick to your finger when poked.

5. Preheat the oil to about 375°F (191 °C) in a frying pan, deep fryer, or wok.

6. With an adult's help, place one or two teaspoon-size portions of dough in the hot oil.

7. Cook the dough on both sides until golden brown. This should take about 5 minutes.

8. Use a slotted spoon to remove the cooked dough from the oil. Drain on a paper towel.

Tools, Weapons, and Defense

Before the Europeans arrived, the Sioux made tools from stone, bone, and wood. By carefully selecting stones and chipping away at them, the Sioux made stone knives, scrapers, and arrowheads.

The Sioux also made tools from every part of the bison. Bison hides provided shelter and clothing, the meat was eaten, and other parts were used to make tools. Knives, scrapers, drills, and needles were made from bison bones. Cups and bowls were made from bison horns, while bags and containers were made from bison organs.

Before the Sioux had horses, they used dogs as pack animals. The Sioux attached two poles to the dog's shoulders to form an A-shaped frame. The poles dragged on the ground, and skins held them together. This device was called a **travois**. Belongings that needed to be transported were piled on the skins. When the Sioux began using horses, they created larger travois that could carry more belongings. The travois poles were also used for the tipi.

The Sioux made buffalo hide shields from the thick hide found at the buffalo's neck.

WAR AND HUNTING

The Sioux were excellent hunters and brave warriors. They used lances, or spears, and bows and arrows to hunt bison and other wild animals. These hunting weapons were also used as weapons of war.

Before guns arrived on the Great Plains, the bow and arrow was the main weapon used by the Sioux. To make bows, willow branches were boiled, shaped, and dried into a near half-circle shape. The Sioux made **arrowheads** from rocks that had been carefully chipped and shaped to a point. **Sinew**, a tough tissue that connects muscles to bones, connected the arrowhead to a willow branch shaft. Feathers were attached to the end of the willow shaft to help it fly straight. An animal hide grip allowed the warrior or hunter to hold the bow tightly while aiming the arrow.

The Sioux and other Plains Indians used shields made from animal hides. Symbols decorated the shields. The Sioux believed these symbols would help protect a warrior in battle.

Europeans introduced new weapons, including guns, to the Sioux. Guns and swift horses helped make the Sioux fearless warriors. Guns also made it easier for the Sioux to hunt bison.

Bison hide was also used to construct quivers, containers that hold arrows.

Sioux Religion

Religion was an important part of the Sioux's everyday life. The Sioux believed every living thing had a spirit. All creatures and things on Earth were connected and depended on one another.

Wakan Tanka, or the Great Spirit, was the most important spirit. The Sioux believed the Great Spirit existed at the beginning of time and created all living things. The Great Spirit also created the Sun, the Moon, and the stars.

Each tribe had at least one medicine man or woman. The Sioux believed that medicine men and women were either born with the ability to communicate with spirits or learned it at an early age. Medicine men and women were highly respected in the

The Sioux believed a medicine person could communicate with the spirit world. Since the Sioux believed spirits caused illness, the medicine person was also a healer.

WACIPI

community because the Sioux believed they had the power to control spirits and cure illnesses.

Today, medicine men and women continue to serve in important roles throughout American Indian communities. They help keep American Indian history and language alive and provide mental and spiritual healing. They also continue to heal people in Sioux communities using traditional medicines. Medicine men and women are still respected for their knowledge and wisdom.

By 1883, the U.S. government had banned traditional Sioux rituals and practices. Despite these laws, some tribes secretly celebrated their traditional dances and ceremonies. This ban was lifted in 1933, when tribes began joining together to rebuild their culture. This joining together marked the beginning of the present-day wacipi.

Each year, wacipi celebrations are held between March and September. Wacipi include singing, dancing, and visiting with friends and family.

Ceremonies and Celebrations

The Sioux performed many rituals, religious ceremonies, and celebrations. At these events, men and women performed songs and special dances.

One of the most important ceremonies was the Sun Dance. The Sun Dance took place each year during the **summer solstice**. At this time of year, many tribes came together to hunt bison. During the Sun Dance, dancers **fasted**. They pierced the flesh on their chests or their backs with wooden skewers. Using leather cords, the skewers were attached to the top of the Sun Dance pole in the center of the Sun Dance lodge. The dancers sang,

In the winter, when the ground was frozen, the Sioux could not bury bodies in a grave. Instead, they wrapped the bodies in a blanket and placed them on burial platforms.

prayed, and danced around the Sun Dance pole, hoping for a vision. After many hours, the dancers broke free of the cords that tied them to the Sun Dance pole. This caused their skin to tear. The Sioux considered this dance a brave act. They believed the courage of these men pleased the spirits. This ensured that the spirits would protect everyone in the community throughout the coming year.

Another religious practice, which Sioux boys, and sometimes girls, participated in as they matured was a **vision quest**. A vision quest lasted 4 days. The young person traveled to a distant place and prayed for a vision of a spirit. This spirit became the boy's or girl's guardian.

The Sioux spent the first 3 days of the 4-day Sun Dance ceremony selecting the tall, straight tree that would be used as the Sun Dance pole.

The sacred pipe played an important role in Sioux life. The Sioux believed the pipe was a gift from the Great Spirit. A representative of the Great Spirit named the White Buffalo Calf Woman first brought the pipe to the Sioux. She taught them how to use the pipe to send messages to the spirits. Sioux men smoked the pipe at important spiritual events, such as daily prayers, the Sun Dance, or vision quests. The smoke carried prayers to the spirits, Earth, and the four cardinal points of the compass—north, south, east, and west. The Sioux believed the Great Spirit gave each cardinal point a sacred power. The Sioux faced each direction when they prayed with the pipe so their message would reach the sacred power at that point.

Music and Dance

Music has always been an important part of Sioux culture. Music is performed during dances and celebrations. Songs and music differ from one region to the next, and have changed over time. In 1889, a Paiute Indian named Wovoka founded a new religion called the Ghost Dance. The religion quickly spread to the Sioux. Elaborate dances and special songs are an important part of the Ghost Dance. Many people wrote songs for the Ghost Dance and some became well known among the Sioux. The songs told about a time when American Indians would regain control of America. The Ghost Dance religion, songs, and ceremonies were banned in 1890. The U.S. government feared the message the religion was spreading.

The present-day wacipi originated during the rebuilding of American Indian culture in the 1930s. Wacipi today are a celebration and coming together of people for dancing, music, crafts, food, and fun. Dancers move to the drumbeat and sometimes compete for prizes.

The Sioux hand drum has a wooden frame with thick rawhide stretched over both sides.

CEREMONIAL DANCING

One type of dance the Sioux perform at a wacipi is the Jingle Dress Dance. This dance was created in the 1920s. Dancers wear traditional clothing with detailed beadwork and feathers as they participate in the traditional Jingle Dress Dance. They wear dresses made of cloth covered with hundreds of small metal cones. As the dancers move to the beat of the music, the metal cones jingle. Men and women, young and old, take part in the dances. Spectators may join in during the intertribal dance. As was customary long ago, people attending wacipi today must be respectful and considerate of one another.

When they perform the Fancy Dance, women wear a detailed knee-length dress, beaded moccasins with matching leggings, and a fancy shawl.

Sioux of all ages participate in ceremonial dancing.

Language and Storytelling

The Dakota, Lakota, and Nakota Sioux speak different dialects of the same language. This means that the words themselves or the organization of words are similar, but the pronunciation or spelling may be different. For example, the Dakota word for "thank you" is *pidamiye*. The Lakota word for "thank you" is *pilamiye*. The Nakota word for "thank you" is *pinamiye*. By studying the Sioux language and its dialects, it is possible to understand how the Dakota, Lakota, and Nakota people and their languages are related. The dialects also help to show how the Sioux language changed over time.

Stories and traditions are passed on by Sioux storytellers or Sioux chanters.

American Indians of the Great Plains did not have a written alphabet. They passed on their history in a number of ways, including painting images on bison hides, painting or carving pictures into rocks, and telling stories. Storytelling was used to teach and entertain. Elders often gathered the young people around a fire to tell stories and legends. Children listened and were taught proper behavior, tribal customs, and family history. To test their memory, children might be asked to repeat the stories, some of which may have taken several evenings to tell.

The Sioux, like many other Plains Indians, also used sign language to communicate. Sign language uses hand gestures and movement to express actions and ideas. Sign language was very useful for communicating with members from other tribes who spoke different dialects and languages.

The Sioux used the art of hide painting to create painted hide robes.

Sioux Art

The Sioux used materials they found in nature to decorate everyday items and create art. They made dyes out of plants or minerals. They also made beads from porcupine quills and seeds.

The Sioux did not have a written language, so their history was passed on through stories and painted images. Sioux historians painted important events on a piece of hide, which was called winter count. The historians passed on the meaning of the painted pictures so that no one would forget what they meant.

Many Indian tribes throughout North America also recorded tribal events on rock. Pictures painted on rocks are called pictographs. Rock carvings are called petroglyphs. Daily life, important events, hunting scenes, or visions were recorded using these methods. Pictographs and petroglyphs that are

The Sioux created Spirit Dolls out of decorated animal hide and feathers. The Sioux also painted artwork and stories on elk hides.

thousands of years old have been found on cave walls, cliffs, and large boulders throughout the Great Plains. While it is very difficult to determine when some of the pictographs and petroglyphs were made, many pre-date the Sioux's arrival on the Great Plains. The Sioux believed these images were sacred.

Before the Sioux began living on the Great Plains, they lived in the area that is now Minnesota. Here, they made pottery containers, which they used for cooking and storage. However, as the Sioux moved farther west, pottery became too heavy to carry long distances. The Sioux began using **parfleches** to store things because they were light and easy to carry. They often decorated parfleches with detailed and beautiful designs.

Today, many Sioux earn an income as artists. Some Sioux artists create paintings, sculptures, bronzes, or photographs to express themselves and to teach people about their culture and way of life.

DECORATION

Decoration added color to moccasins, clothing, and ceremonial objects. Women spent many hours creating quill and beadwork designs on scraped and prepared animal hides. Women often decorated hides with thin, hollow porcupine quills. They pulled quills from the dead animal, organized them by size, and dyed the quills different colors. Quills could be up to 4 inches (10 cm) long. Each tribe had its own style of decoration and design. Certain colors or shapes, such as triangles or rectangles, might be more important to one tribe than to another. When European traders arrived, Sioux women began using glass beads in their work. The Sioux valued glass beads because they did not require preparation, came in brilliant colors, and sparkled in the sunlight.

Sitting Bull

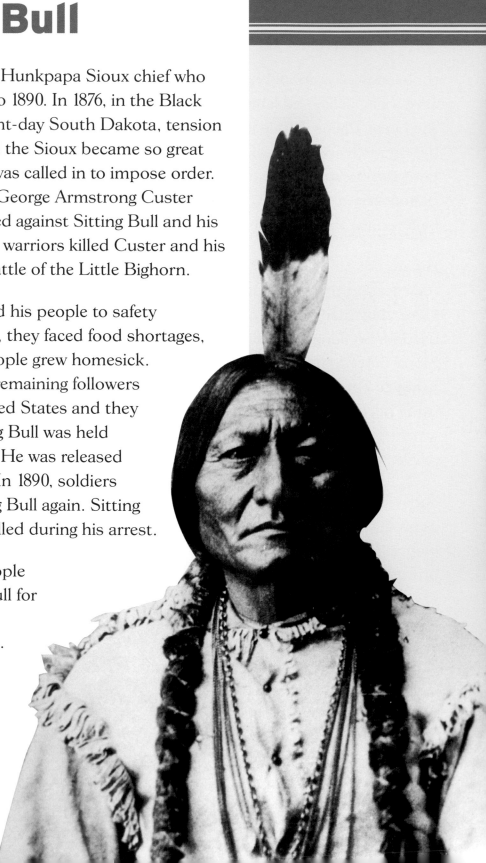

Sitting Bull was a Hunkpapa Sioux chief who lived from 1831 to 1890. In 1876, in the Black Hills region of present-day South Dakota, tension between settlers and the Sioux became so great that the U.S. Army was called in to impose order. Lieutenant Colonel George Armstrong Custer and his troops battled against Sitting Bull and his followers. The Sioux warriors killed Custer and his troops during the Battle of the Little Bighorn.

Later, Sitting Bull led his people to safety in Canada. However, they faced food shortages, and Sitting Bull's people grew homesick. Sitting Bull and his remaining followers returned to the United States and they were arrested. Sitting Bull was held prisoner for 2 years. He was released from prison in 1885. In 1890, soldiers tried to arrest Sitting Bull again. Sitting Bull was shot and killed during his arrest.

Today, the Sioux people remember Sitting Bull for his wise leadership, bravery, and courage.

In 1953, Sitting Bull's remains were moved to Mobridge, South Dakota.

MODERN ARTIST

Donald F. Montileaux

Donald F. Montileaux is a Sioux painter. He is a member of the Oglala Lakota Tribe. He was born in Pine Ridge, South Dakota, in 1948. He is married and has three children. Montileaux taught himself to paint. However, he has since attended the Institute of American Indian Art in Santa Fe, New Mexico. Here, he studied under Oscar Howe, a well-known artist. Hide painter Herman Red Elk was Montileaux's **mentor** and most important influence.

Montileaux describes himself as a storyteller. His paintings depict the traditional Lakota way of life. They feature hunters and warriors on horseback, as well as other ancient and modern themes. Montileaux's

Montileaux uses acrylic paints. He paints on canvas, paper, and hides.

work is influenced by tipi and hide paintings of the past. The flat images and primary colors of his paintings are based on traditional Lakota art.

Montileaux has won many awards for his paintings. He has exhibited his work in art shows across the United States. Many of his paintings hang in private and public collections, including the Institute of American Indian Art in Santa Fe, New Mexico, and the Sioux Indian Museum in Rapid City, South Dakota. Montileaux was honored when one of his paintings traveled around the Earth aboard the space shuttle *Endeavor* in 1995.

Montileaux currently works as a marketing consultant, helping other Native artists show and sell their work. In addition, he has taught arts and crafts in places such as Spain, where he taught students how to paint tipis.

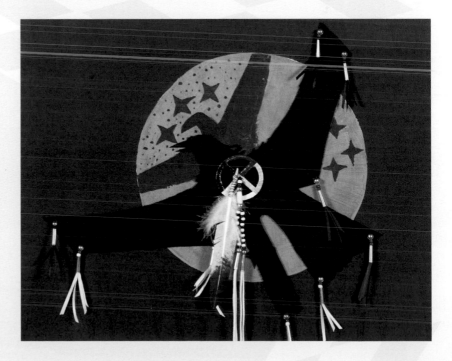

Studying the Sioux's Past

Archaeologists study items left by cultures from the past. The Sioux left many **artifacts** behind. From these artifacts, archaeologists can learn more about how the Sioux lived.

Scientists have discovered that before the Europeans brought metal cooking pots to the Great Plains, the Sioux cooked foods, such as stew, in bison stomachs. They heated rocks in a fire and then placed the rocks in the stew. The heat from the rocks cooked the stew. If the rocks were heated and cooled many times, they broke. These rocks are called **fire broken rock**.

Archaeologists have also found stone circles called **tipi rings** on the Great Plains. These stones helped hold down the base of the tipi. When the Sioux moved to a new location, they packed up their tipis and left the stones behind.

Archaeologists have found Sioux artifacts, such as stone and bone tools, arrowheads, and hearths, too.

Some painted bison hides told stor using pictures.

Red pipestone is quarried in Pipestone, Minnesota. The Sioux consider these quarries sacred places. They collect stone from these areas to makes pipes and other items.

Initial Woodland Tradition 200 B.C. – A.D. 500

Sioux ancestors lived in the area now known as Minnesota; made pottery containers and earthen burial mounds.

Terminal Woodland Tradition A.D. 500 – 1680

Sioux ancestors continued to make pottery, gather wild rice, and hunt deer and elk; made houses using wooden posts, bark, and dirt.

First recorded contact with Europeans 1659 – 1660

Pierre Radisson recorded meeting the Sioux in the Minnesota region.

Gradual westward migration begins Circa 1680

The Sioux moved to the eastern Dakotas.

Living on the Great Plains Late 1700s

The Sioux now live in the Dakotas, Wyoming, and eastern Montana; the Sioux began riding horses.

Disappearance of bison 1870s – 1880s

Great Plains bison are almost hunted to extinction.

The Sioux made rattles by covering a wooden handle with rawhide. They filled the top of the rattle with seeds or small stones to make sound.

Make Your Own Parfleche Bag

Parfleches were rawhide containers. The Sioux used them to hold food, clothing, and other items. They were decorated with colorful designs. Parfleches were light and easy to carry. You can make your own parfleche container. While this parfleche will not be made of rawhide, it will give you a good idea how a parfleche was created and decorated. Your parfleche will be folded much like a large envelope.

You will need:

- One piece of 11-inch by 17-inch (28-cm by 43-cm) beige or light brown construction paper
- One 12-inch (30-cm) piece of leather or regular string
- Felt markers or crayons
- Scissors
- Hole punch
- 4 reinforcements

Steps

1. Use the diagram below as a guide for cutting the construction paper into the shape of the parfleche bag.
2. Cut along the dark lines to remove a 2-inch by 4-inch (5 cm by 10 cm) section of each corner of the paper.
3. Using a hole punch, punch out two holes on the C flaps, near the edge of the paper. The string will be threaded through these holes.
4. Along the dotted line, fold the A flaps toward each other.
5. Along the dotted line, fold the B flaps toward the C flaps.

6. Fold the C flaps toward and on top of the A flaps.
7. Loop the string through the holes and tie by making a bow. You may need to use reinforcements on the holes to prevent the paper from tearing.
8. Plains Indians would often decorate the outside of flaps A or C in colorful geometric designs. Decorate your parfleche using felt markers or crayons.

	A	
B		B
C		C
B		B
	A	

1"
2"
4"

Further Reading

The Sioux: Nomadic Buffalo Hunters (Blue Earth Books: America's First People) by Rachel A. Koestler-Grack, Bridgestone Books, 2003, explores the traditional life of the Sioux.

For a colorful look at the religion, history, and culture of the Sioux, read *What Do We Know About the Plains Indians?* by Dr. Colin Taylor, Simon and Schuster Young Books, 1993.

Web Sites

Learn about the Oglala Sioux tribe at:
www.lakotamall.com/oglalasiouxtribe/index.htm

Learn about Sitting Bull at:
www.historychannel.com/exhibits/sioux/sittingbull.html

Read different Sioux Indian legends at:
www.indianlegend.com/sioux/sioux_index.htm

GLOSSARY

archaeologists: scientists who study objects from the past to learn about people who lived long ago

arrowheads: the pointed head or striking tip of arrows made of stone or metal

artifacts: objects used or made by humans long ago

bison: a large animal that roams the Great Plains of North America

dialects: changes in a language that is spoken from place to place

fasted: did not consume food or drink

fire broken rock: rock that has been heated and cooled many times during the process of cooking

mentor: a trusted counselor or teacher

moccasins: soft shoes worn by many American Indian groups

nomadic: to move from place to place

parfleches: animal hide containers

reservations: areas of land set aside for American Indians to live on if they choose

sinew: a tough tissue attaching muscle to bone, often used for sewing

summer solstice: the time of year when the Sun is at its most northern point; usually June 21.

Sun Dance: a ceremony involving dancing, singing, and fasting

tanning: a process of cleaning and preparing an animal hide for use

tipis: dwellings made of tree poles and bison hides

tipi rings: stone circles left on the ground after a tipi has been taken down

travois: an A-shaped sled used to carry objects; can be pulled by people, horses, or dogs.

vision quest: a time to pray and seek supernatural guidance

wacipi: American Indian dance festivals involving singing, dancing, and drumming

INDEX